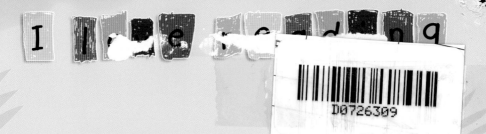
I like reading

Dinosaur Giants

by Monica Hughes

Consultant: Dougal Dixon

Copyright © **ticktock Entertainment Ltd 2007**
First published in Great Britain in 2007 by **ticktock Media Ltd.,**
Unit 2, Orchard Business Centre, North Farm Road, Tunbridge Wells, Kent TN2 3XF

We would like to thank: Shirley Bickler and Suzanne Baker

ISBN 978 1 84696 606 4 pbk
Printed in China

Picture credits
t=top, b=bottom, c=centre, l-left, r=right, OFC= outside front cover
Lisa Alderson: 1, 6-7, 12-13; John Alston: 6l, 8, 20l; Natural History Museum: 17c;
Bob Nicholls: 16-17, 23b; Luis Rey: 2, 4, 5b, 14-15, 18-19, 20-21, 23t, 23c, 23b;
Science Photo Library: 9; Shutterstock: 5t, 14bl, 14br, 19b, 20b; Simon Mendez:
10-11, 22t.

CONTENTS

Dinosaur giants

Long ago dinosaurs and other giant creatures lived on land.

There were giant creatures in the sea and there were giant creatures in the air too.

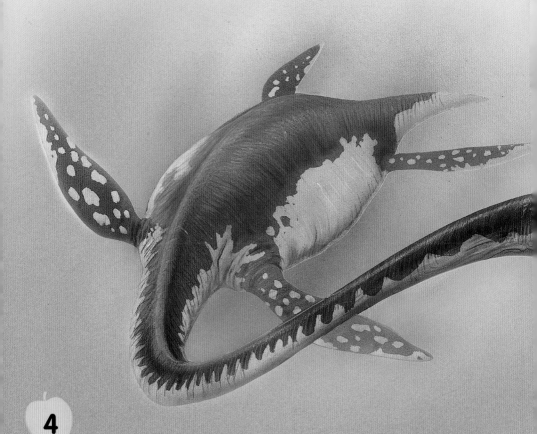

The heaviest meat-eating dinosaur

T. rex may have been the heaviest meat-eater.

Dinosaur size

It weighed about the same as
two large elephants.

T. rex ate large and small animals.

Tyrannosaurus rex
tie-ran-o-sor-us rex

The biggest meat-eating dinosaur

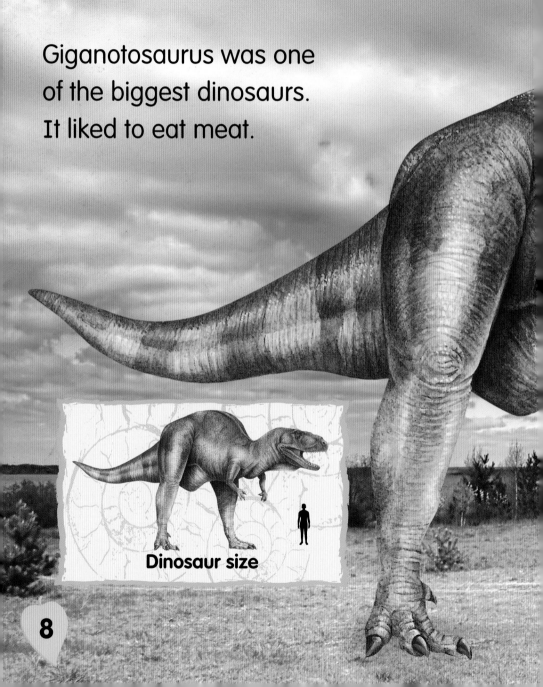

Giganotosaurus was one
of the biggest dinosaurs.
It liked to eat meat.

Dinosaur size

It was 15 metres from its nose to its tail.

This dinosaur was longer than T. rex, but it was not as heavy.

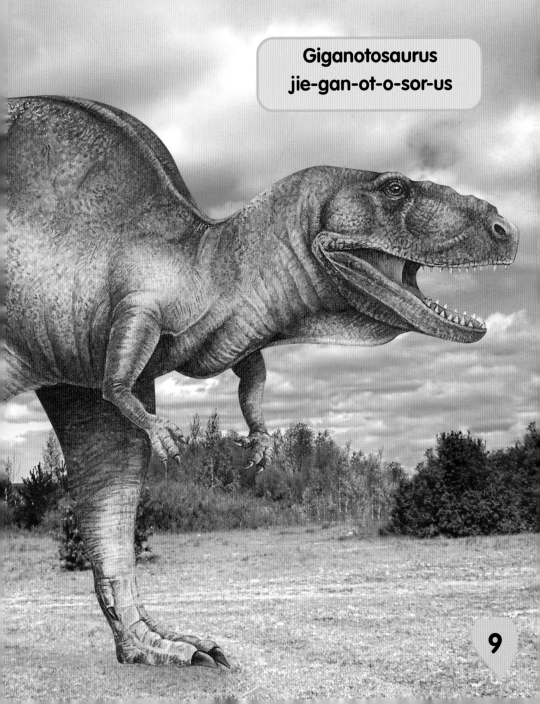

Giganotosaurus
jie-gan-ot-o-sor-us

The heaviest plant-eating dinosaur

This dinosaur was the heaviest dinosaur that ate plants.

It weighed about the same as 14 elephants!

It had a small head and a small brain.

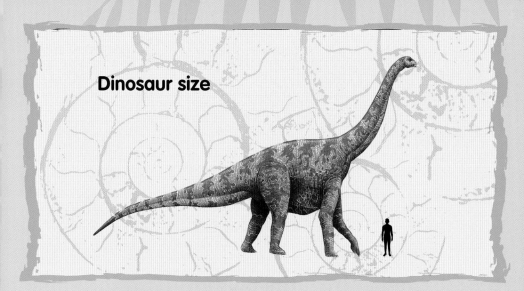

Dinosaur size

Argentinosaurus was about 27 metres long.

Argentinosaurus
ar-jun-teen-o-sor-us

The tallest plant-eating dinosaur

This dinosaur was the tallest dinosaur that ate plants.

It was 22 metres tall and its neck was 16 metres long.

Sauroposeidon
saw-ro-po-si-don

Tail

It had a small head, thick legs and a short tail.

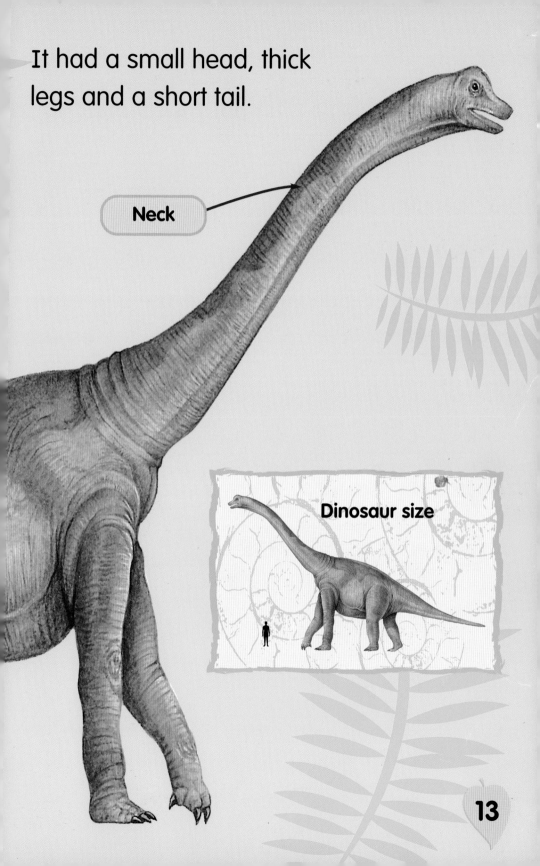

Neck

Dinosaur size

The biggest flying creature

This was the biggest flying creature.

It was as big as a small aeroplane.

It had a long neck and very long jaws.

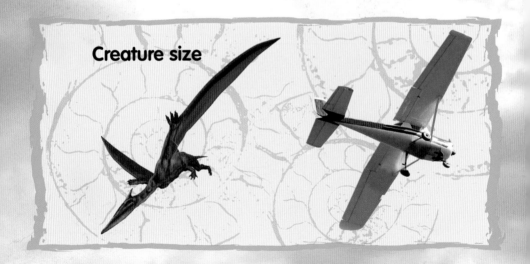

Creature size

It had a big crest on its head.

Crest

Jaws

Quetzalcoatlus
ket-sal-koat-lus

The biggest sea creature

This was the biggest sea creature.

It was 24 metres long with
a big head and a short neck.

Liopleurodon
lee-o-plur-o-don

It had long jaws and
sharp teeth. It was fierce!

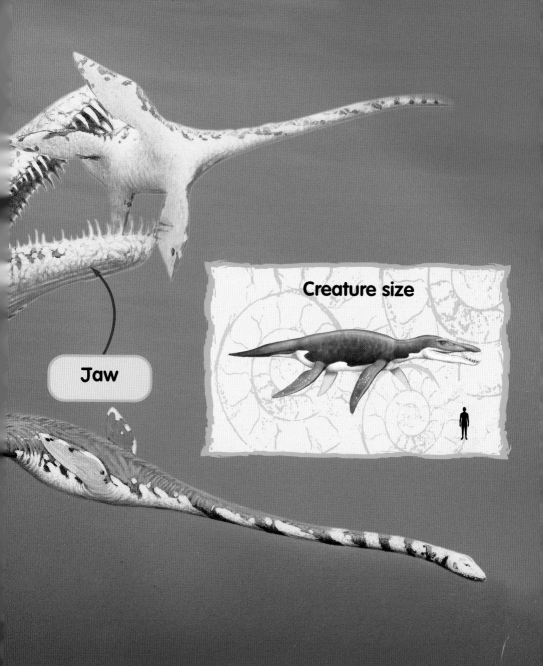

Jaw

Creature size

The sea creature with the longest neck

Look at this creature's long, long neck.
It is much longer than a giraffe's neck.

This giant was 14 metres from its nose to the tip of its tail. Its neck was over seven metres long.

Elasmosaurus
ee-las-mo-sor-us

Creature size

The biggest crocodile?

This monster lived at the time of the dinosaurs. It was the biggest crocodile that has ever lived.

Deinosuchus was 15 metres long.

Creature size

Deinosuchus

Crocodile

It had a long jaw and lots of teeth.
It was so big it could eat a dinosaur!

Deinosuchus
dyn-o-soo-cus

True or false?

T. rex was a dinosaur that ate plants.

True or false?

Liopleurodon was the longest sea creature.

True or false?

Deinosuchus lived at the time of the dinosaurs.

True or false?

Quetzalcoatlus had a big crest on its head.

True or false?

A giraffe has a longer neck than Elasmosaurus.

True or false?

Activities

What did you think of this book?

 Brilliant   **Good**   **OK**

Which page did you like best? Why?

• • • • • • • • • • • • •

Which of these can fly?

Tyrannosaurus rex • Quetzalcoatlus • Sauroposeidon

• • • • • • • • • • • • •

Draw a big picture with dinosaurs and other creatures on the land. Label each creature.

• • • • • • • • • • • • •

Who is the author of this book? Have you read *Dinosaur Battles* by the same author?